FOUNDRYMAN MCQ

OBJECTIVE QUESTION ANSWERS

MANOJ DOLE

Copyright © Manoj Dole
All Rights Reserved.

This book has been published with all efforts taken to make the material error-free after the consent of the author. However, the author and the publisher do not assume and hereby disclaim any liability to any party for any loss, damage, or disruption caused by errors or omissions, whether such errors or omissions result from negligence, accident, or any other cause.

While every effort has been made to avoid any mistake or omission, this publication is being sold on the condition and understanding that neither the author nor the publishers or printers would be liable in any manner to any person by reason of any mistake or omission in this publication or for any action taken or omitted to be taken or advice rendered or accepted on the basis of this work. For any defect in printing or binding the publishers will be liable only to replace the defective copy by another copy of this work then available.

Digitization is the need of the time. In the future, training in industrial training institutes will need to be conducted using online internet to make training more convenient and easy. E-books containing a set of MCQ questions will be made available to the trainees as they need to be more accustomed to the multiple choice questions MCQ to prepare for the online exams taking place in their industrial training institutes.

With all these factors in mind, Mr. Manoj Madhukar Dole Instructor, Industrial Training Institute, Satara, has written books according to the new annual system and NSQF-5 syllabus. And they've created theoretical mobile apps and blogs to make training easier, and made all these educational materials available for download on the world famous websites Google Play Store, Amazon and Apple Book Store.

The books were published by Hon'ble Joint Director Shri Rajendra Ghume Saheb Regional Office of Vocational Education and Training, Pune on 9/1/2019, at this time Shri Prakash Saigavkar Saheb Principal Government Industrial Training Institute Aundh Pune, Shri Tukaram Misal Saheb Principal Govt. Q. Sanstha Satara, Shri Sachin Dhumal Saheb District Vocational Education and Training Officer Satara, Shri Yatin Pargaonkar Saheb Principal Govt. Q. Sanstha Kolhapur, Shri Vikas Teke Saheb Inspector Vocational Education and Training Regional Office Pune, Palekar Foods Products Pvt. Ltd. Entrepreneurial Chairman of Satara Mr. Nilkanthrao Palekar Saheb, Chairman of Hira Foods Mr. Ibrahim Baba Tamboli Saheb, Mrs. Shalmali Pawar Headmaster Government Technical School Center Satara and other dignitaries were present on the occasion.

Contents

Prologue   *vii*

Foreword   *ix*

Preface   *xi*

Acknowledgements   *xiii*

1. Foundryman Qr Code Images   1

Prologue

Foundryman MCQ is a simple e-Book for ITI & Engineering Course Foundryman, Revised NSQ Syllabus in 2022, It contains objective questions with underlined & bold correct answers MCQ covering all topics including all about the latest & Important about broadly covers safety aspect in general to safety aspect specific to the trade, identify tools & equipment, raw materials used in casting. Further sand sieving and mixing, sand testing is taught. Other operations like ramming, channel cutting, sand preparation, backing and gate cutting are covered. In addition, core making, preparation of green sand mould, leveling of floor, bedding in mould, preparing mould with different types of core, preparing differing mould as per equipment are also covered. The related wood working different pattern making are also part of the practical task. Different metal working like chipping, filing, grinding, drilling etc. are also covered. Finally, the melting practice on induction furnace is undertaken. Preparation of different moulds viz., loam sand mould, pit mould, CO2 mould and making casting is covered in the beginning. In addition, preparation of mould with different core setting viz., balancing core, hanging core along with casting different metals are covered. Finding the yield percentage is also part of the practical task. Simultaneously preparation of complete core by joining half core is covered. Further, preparation of mould with different gates viz., pencil, finger, wedge ring, branch, relief sprue, skim bob, horn gate, stepped gate etc. including making casting of different metal is covered. Practical skills like relining different furnace viz., fit, oil fired, muffles are covered along with ladle. The preparations of core by linseed oil and ivpoils, preparing mould without pattern are also part of practical skills. Finally, making cast by die & investment casting are covered and lots more.

We add new question answers with each new version. Please email us in case of any errors/omissions. This is arguably the largest and best e-Book for All engineering multiple choice questions and answers.

As a student you can use it for your exam prep. This e-Book is also useful for professors to refresh material.

Foreword

Vocational education and training is imparted through the Department of Vocational Education and Training through the Department of Business Education and Business Practical to supply multi-skilled artisans in line with the rapidly growing demand in the industrial sector in the 21st century. All the occupations within the institutions are important, as the trainees from these occupations develop multi-skills as per the demands of the industry.

with the noble intention of making available MCQ e-books suitable for all businesses, considering that all the examinations in all the industries in the industrial sector are conducted online and include MCQ method questions. Mr. Manoj Madhukar Dole has written a very good e-book on MCQ method as per the new annual syllabus. This e-book will definitely be a guide for all the trainees, trainee candidates, training instructors and others concerned.

The author of the book is Mr. Manoj Madhukar Dole, Instructor Gov. ITI Satara has 17 years of training experience. Written as a new annual pattern, this e-book incorporates modern digital QR Code technology to understand the layout, simple language, and simple syntax, diagrams and videos for each subject. So I am sure that this e-book will definitely be useful for in-depth study and exam practice. The work they have done is certainly commendable.

Mr. Tukaram Misal
Principal Government Industrial Training Institute Satara.

Preface

DGET New Delhi and CSTARI Kolkata have been implementing an annual pattern for all businesses in ITI since the August 2018 session. The examination system will also be changed and it will be online from this year and since all the questions are of Objective Type (MCQ), the trainees are in dire need of in-depth study. It is with this in mind that we are delighted to present the books based on the old NIMI pattern and a complete overview of the new annual pattern, and we hope that these books will be a guide for all business directors and trainees. Is.

For writing these books, Johar Awate Saheb, Principal of ITI Akluj. Former Principal of ITI Satara Saigavkar Saheb, Assistant Director Shri Chandrakant Dhekne Saheb Regional Office of Vocational Education and Training, Pune, District Vocational Education and Training Officer Sachin Dhumal Saheb and Headmaster Government Technical School Kendra Shalmali Pawar Madam and son Adhiraj Dole, mother Kusum Dole, I am very grateful to my father Madhukar Dole and wife Ashwini Dole for their special guidance and cooperation from time to time.

Also, in a very short period of time, the book was reviewed by Shri Rajendra Ghume Saheb, Joint Director, Vocational Education and Training Regional Office, Pune, for his invaluable time in publishing the book. I am sincerely grateful for their feedback.

I am grateful to the Instructor of ITI Satara for there continuous support from the very beginning of writing the book.

From this book, I consider myself blessed to have shared my thoughts on e-learning with you. I will not claim that this book is perfect, because considering the perfection, this book is an attempt and is in its infancy. They will be valuable for improvement if they are tested and suggested.

Manoj Dole
Dated 9/1/2019

Acknowledgements

The industrial training and theoretical examination system of our industrial training institutes and these changes have been accepted by the craft instructors and the trainees. Theoretical examinations conducted in your industrial training institutes are also conducted online. Since these examinations are of multiple choice MCQ method, the trainees will need to get more practice of such questions.

With all these considerations in mind, Mr. Manoj Madhukar, Director, Dole Crafts, Katari Industrial Training Institute, Satara, has done a thorough study and with his diligent work and added his keen intellect, according to the new annual system and NSQF-5 syllabus, e-book of Katari and other machine trades. -Book) and they have created mobile apps and blogs on theoretical topics to make training easier and have made all these educational materials available for download on the world famous websites Google Play Store, Amazon and Apple Book Store. Training has been made easier by creating a print version and using advanced techniques like QR Code.

All these educational materials will definitely be a guide for all the trainees for in-depth study and for the craft instructors and other concerned who are imparting vocational training.

Foundryman QR Code Images

Download App
Online Test Exam
ITI Books
AutoCAD CAM
JOB & Apprentice
Online Theory
Computer Course
Trading Course
CNC Course
MSCIT Course
Shopping Business
Internet Business
Web Designing
Online Services
Top Sportsmans
Indian Army
Freedom Fighters
Top Scientists
Social Reformers
Motivational Speaker
Top Richest People
Join WhatsApp Group
Join Facebook Group
Like Facebook Page
PAN / Adhar / Licence
Passport

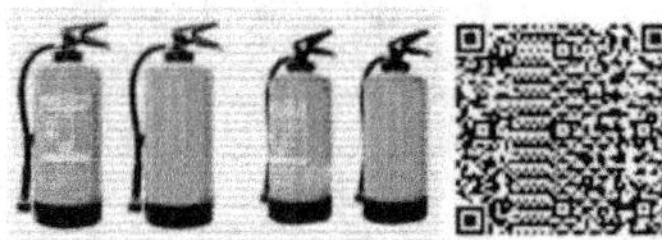

Fire extinguisher

Calliper

Hacksaw frame

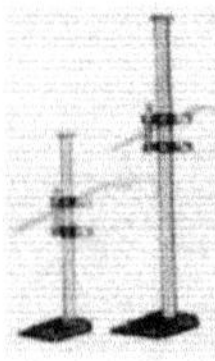

Universal surface guage

Hammer

Centre punch

Bench vice

Files

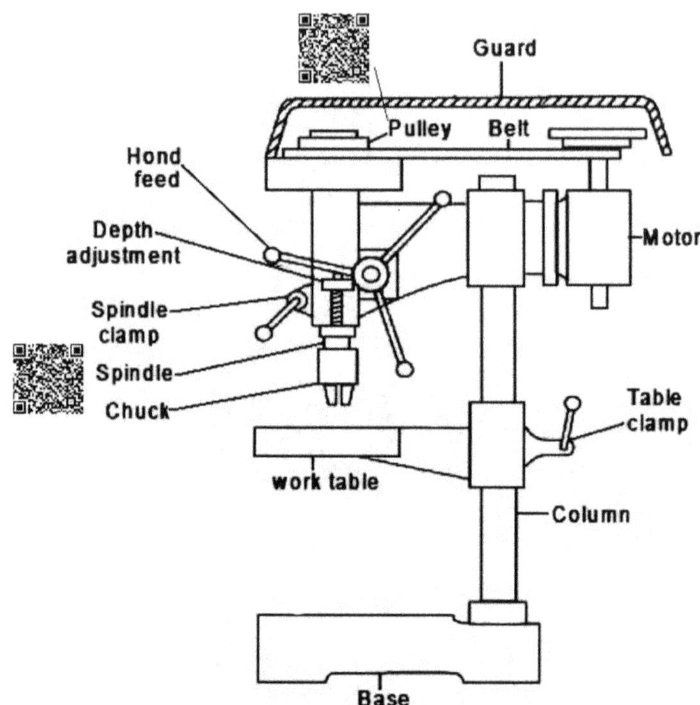

Piller Drilling Machine

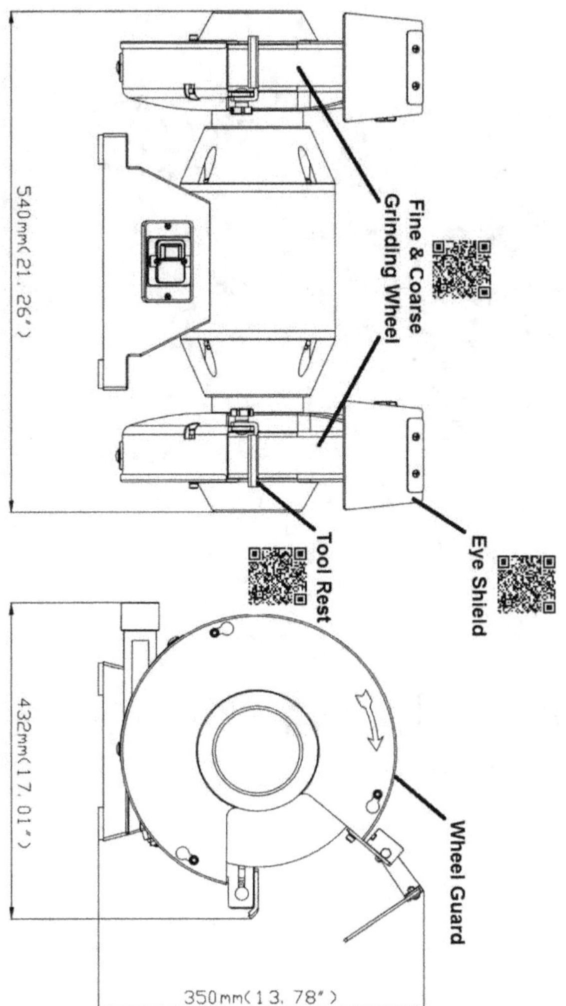
Bench Grinding Machine
540mm(21.26")
Fine & Coarse Grinding Wheel
Eye Shield
Tool Rest
432mm(17.01")
350mm(13.78")
Wheel Guard

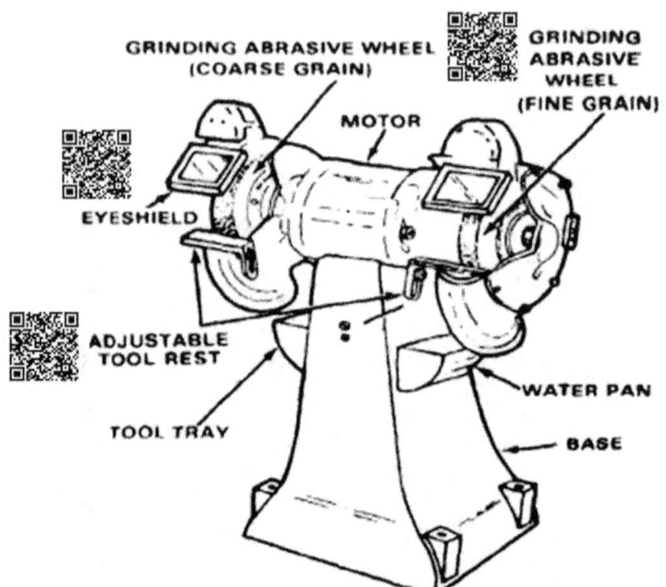

Pedastal Grinding Machine

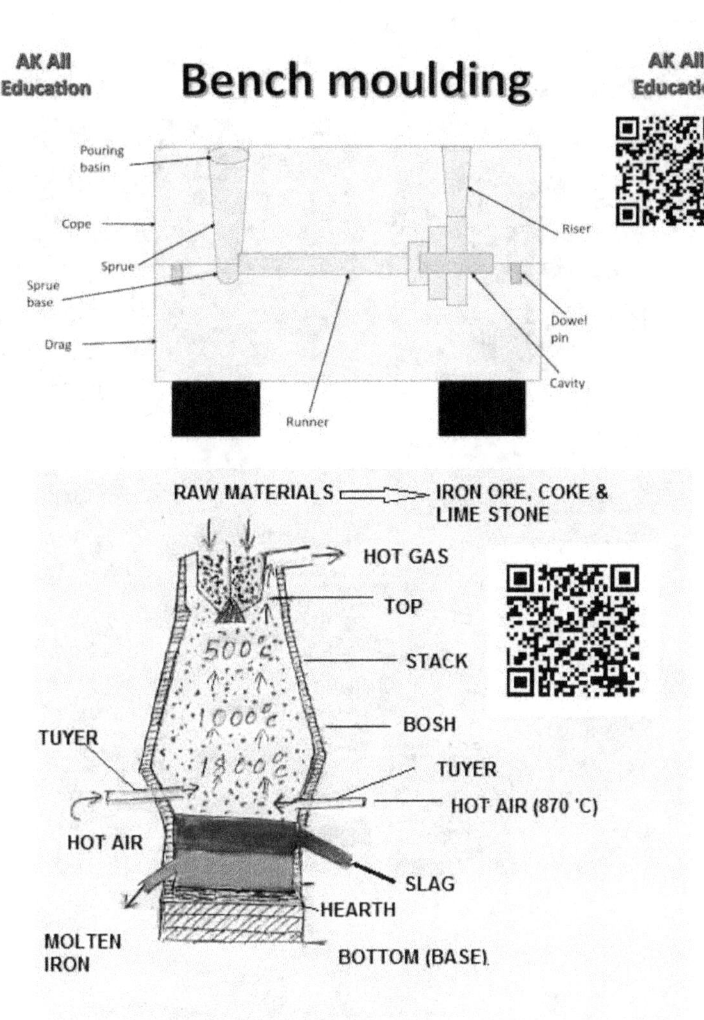
AK All Education
AK All Education
Bench moulding
Pouring basin
Cope
Sprue
Sprue base
Drag
Riser
Dowel pin
Cavity
Runner
RAW MATERIALS IRON ORE, COKE & LIME STONE
HOT GAS
TOP
500°c
STACK
1000°c
BOSH
1800°c
TUYER
TUYER
HOT AIR (870 °C)
HOT AIR
SLAG
HEARTH
MOLTEN IRON
BOTTOM (BASE)
BLAST FURNACE

Cement Bonded Sand Moulding

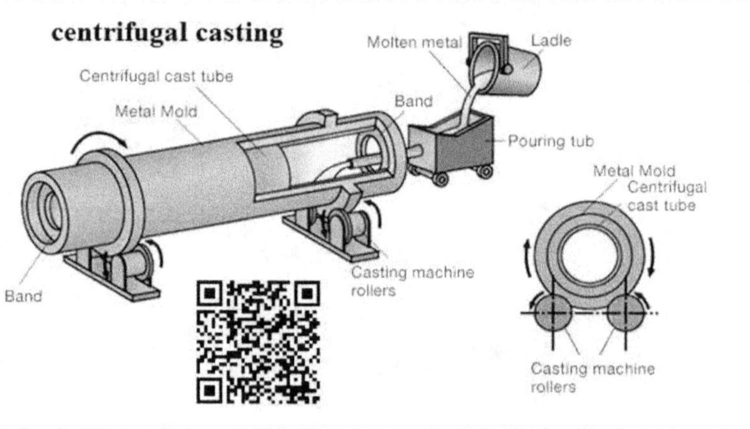

centrifugal casting

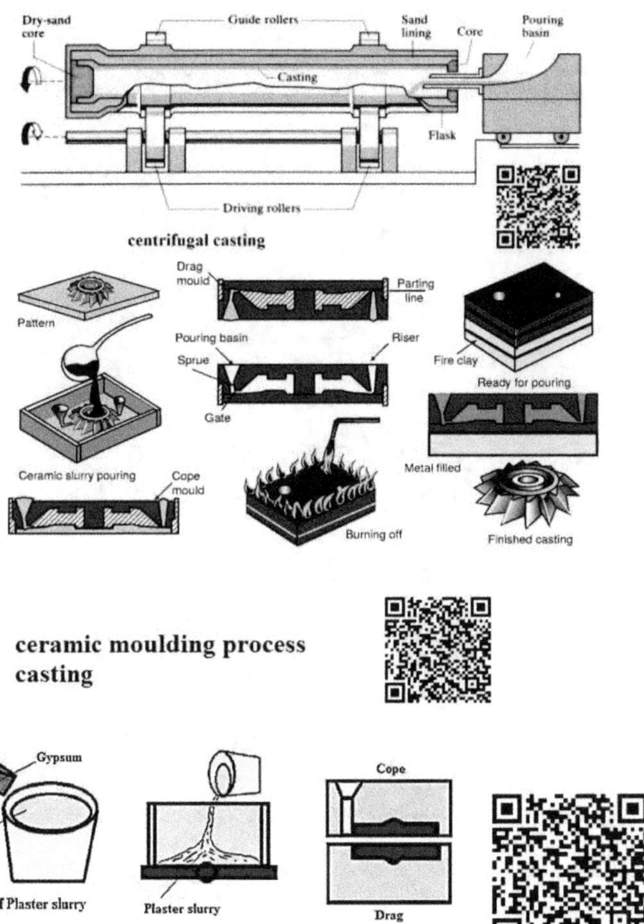

centrifugal casting

ceramic moulding process casting

Fig.1.43 : Ceramic mould making

Internal and External Chills

Figure 10.13 Various types of (a) internal and (b) external chills (dark areas at corners), used in castings to eliminate porosity caused by shrinkage. Chills are placed in regions where there is a larger volume of metals, as shown in (c).

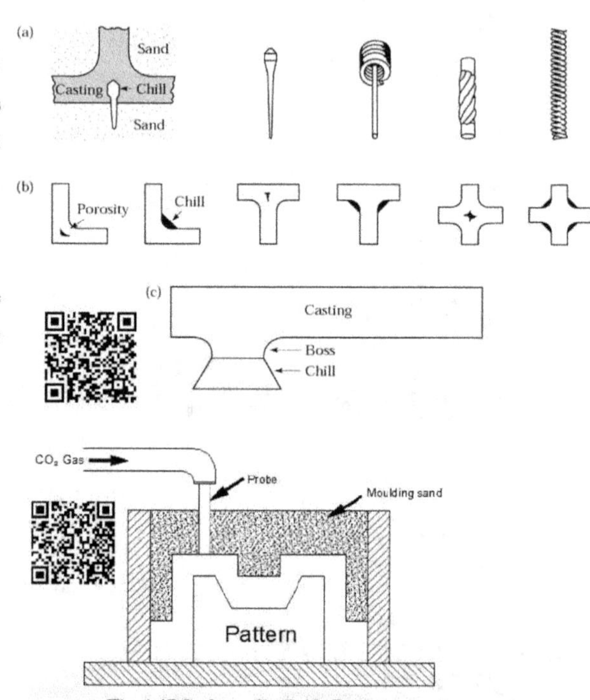

Fig. 1.47 Carbon - di - Oxide Processess

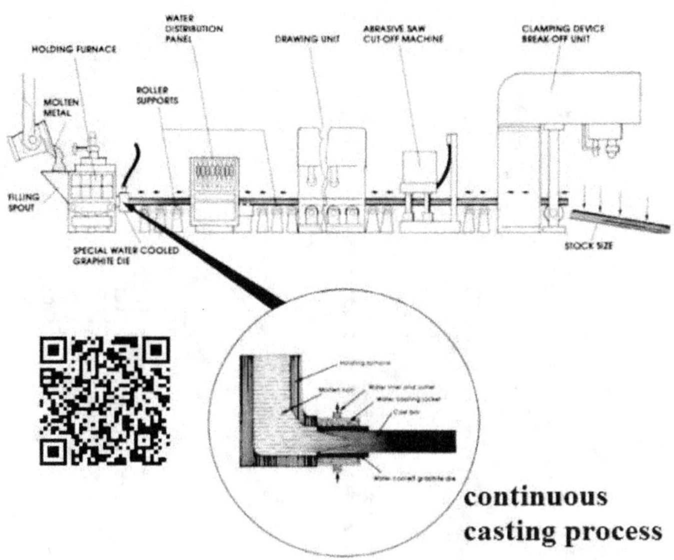

continuous casting process

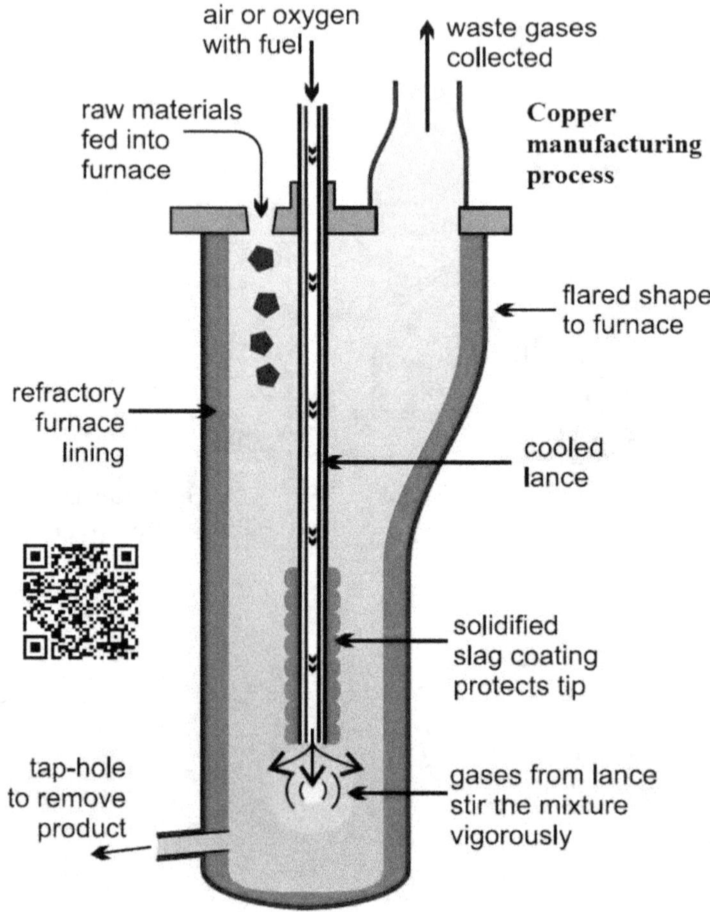

air or oxygen with fuel
waste gases collected
Copper manufacturing process
raw materials fed into furnace
flared shape to furnace
refractory furnace lining
cooled lance
solidified slag coating protects tip
tap-hole to remove product
gases from lance stir the mixture vigorously

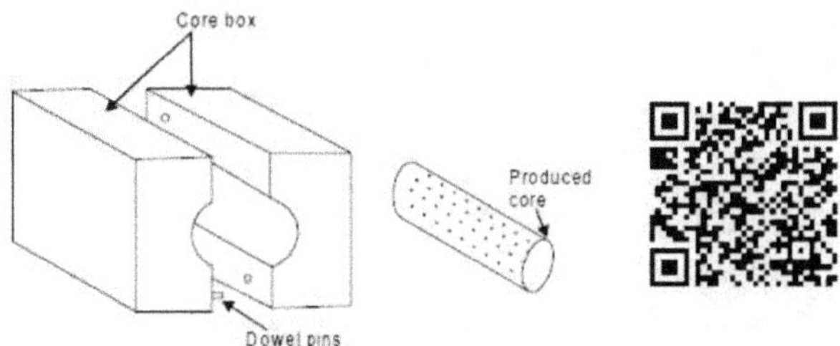

Fig. 10.19   Split core-box

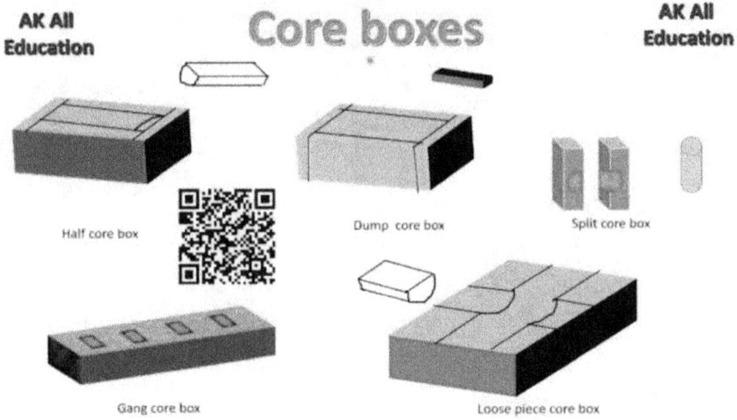

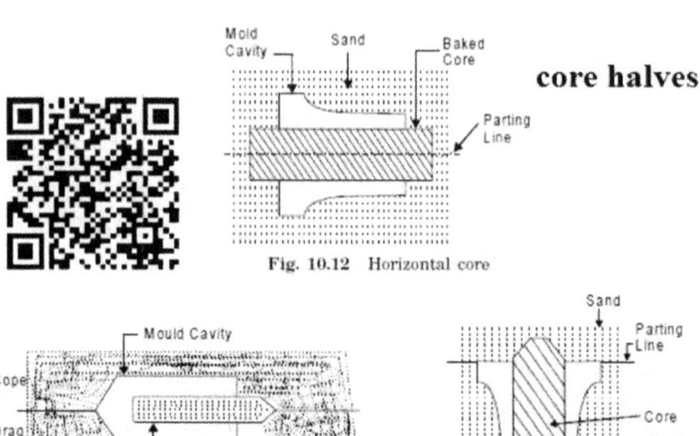

Fig. 10.12   Horizontal core

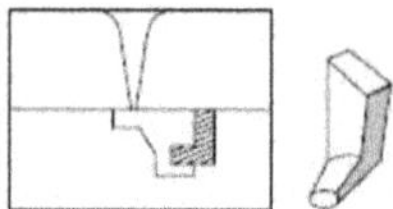

Fig. 10.13   Vertical core

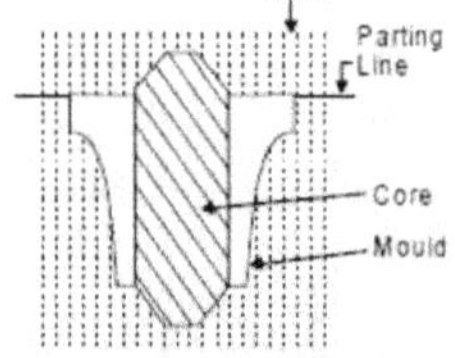

Fig. 10.14   Balanced core

Fig. 10.15   Drop core

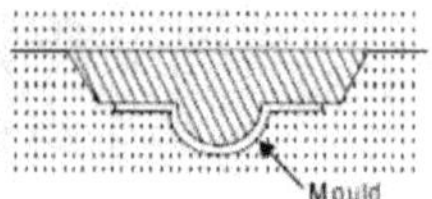

Fig. 10.16   Hanging core

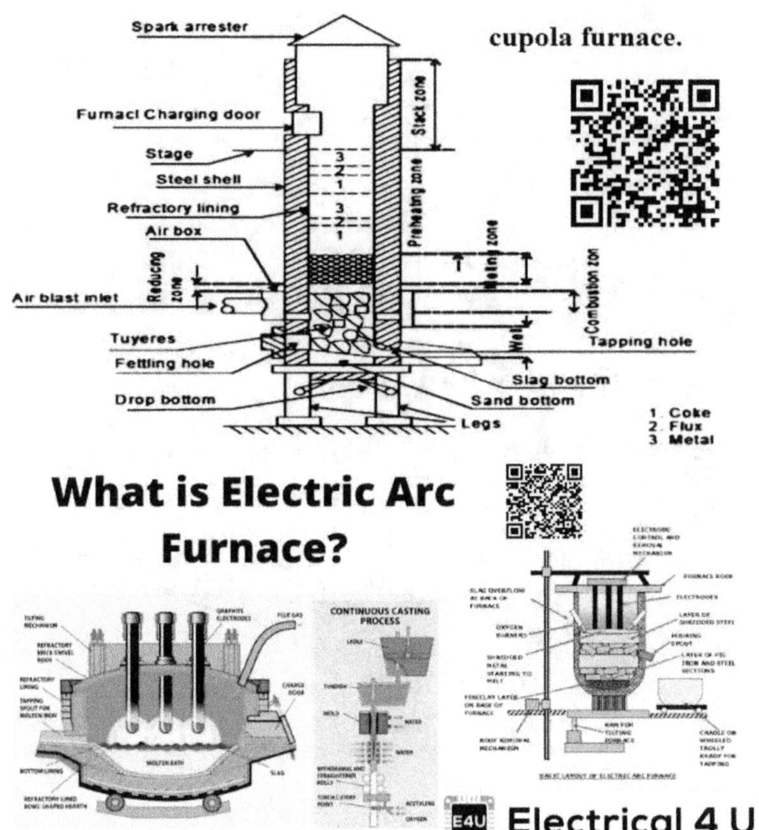

What is Electric Arc Furnace?

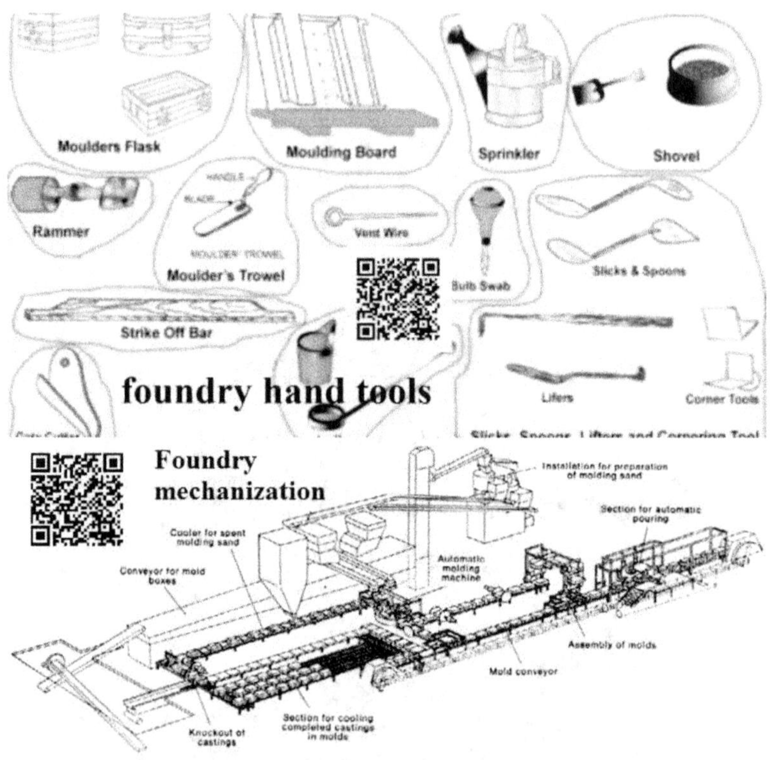
Moulders Flask
Moulding Board
Sprinkler
Shovel
Rammer
HANDLE
BLADE
MOULDERS TROWEL
Moulder's Trowel
Vent Wire
Bulb Swab
Slicks & Spoons
Strike Off Bar
foundry hand tools
Lifters
Corner Tools
Slicks, Spoons, Lifters and Cornering Tool
Foundry mechanization
Installation for preparation of molding sand
Cooler for spent molding sand
Section for automatic pouring
Conveyor for mold boxes
Automatic molding machine
Assembly of molds
Mold conveyor
Knockout of castings
Section for cooling completed castings in molds

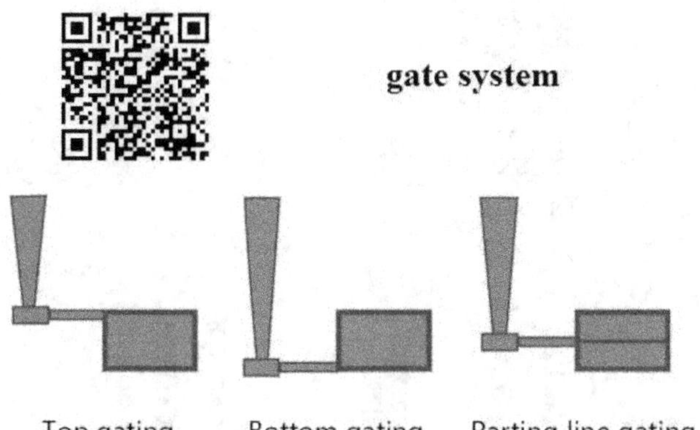

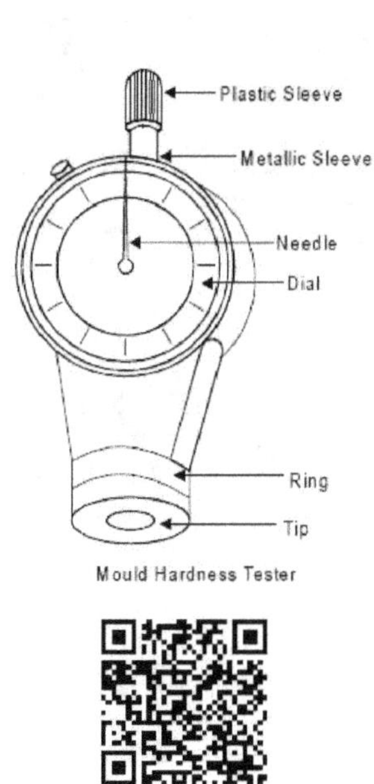

Mould Hardness Tester

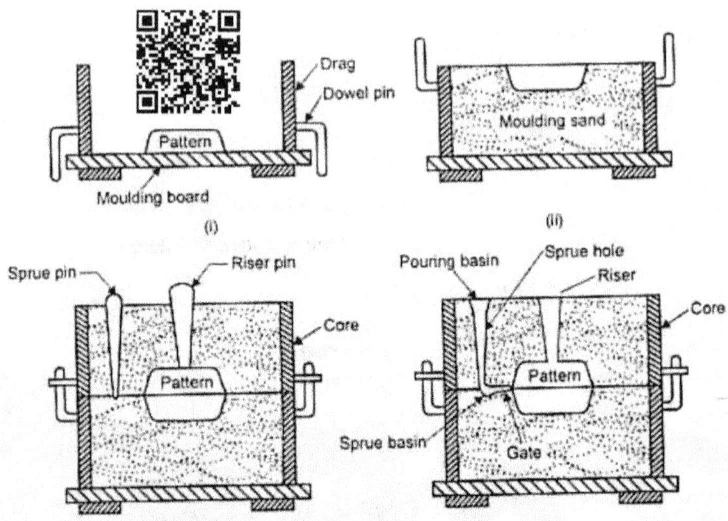

Fig. 1.31 Green sand Moulding Processes

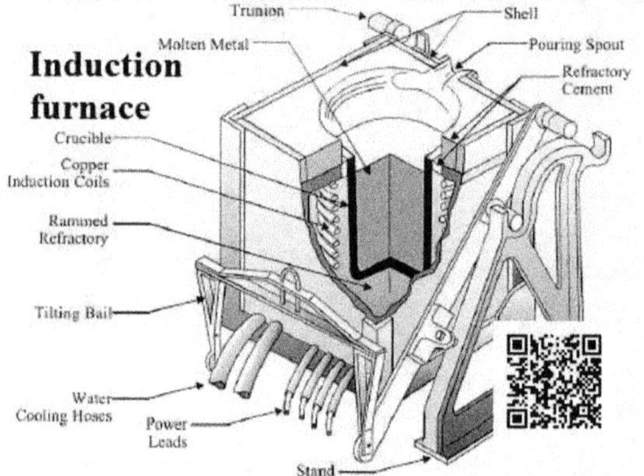

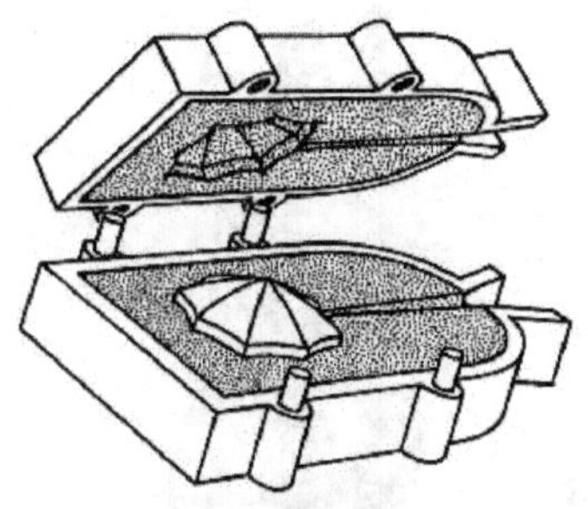

loam sand
mould

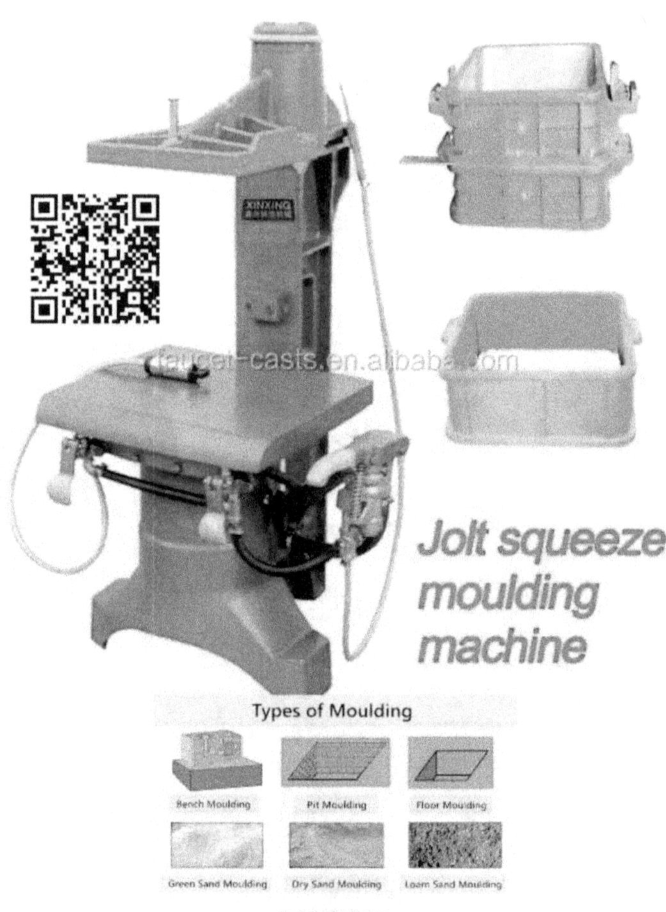

Types of Moulding

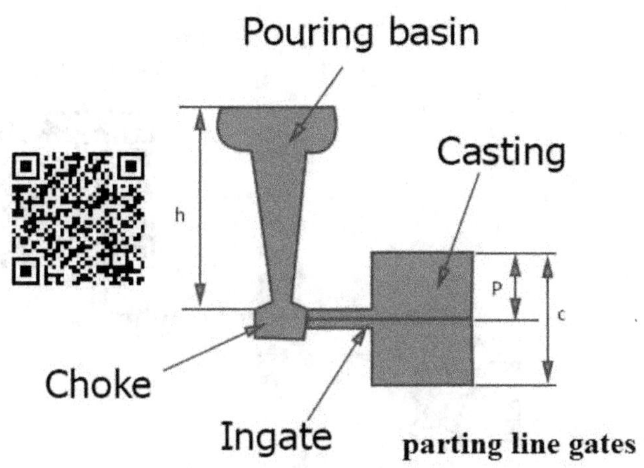
Pouring basin
Casting
h
P
c
Choke
Ingate
parting line gates

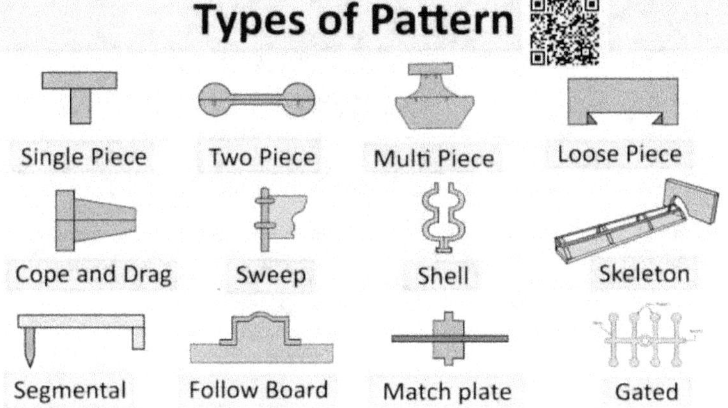
Types of Pattern
Single Piece
Two Piece
Multi Piece
Loose Piece
Cope and Drag
Sweep
Shell
Skeleton
Segmental
Follow Board
Match plate
Gated

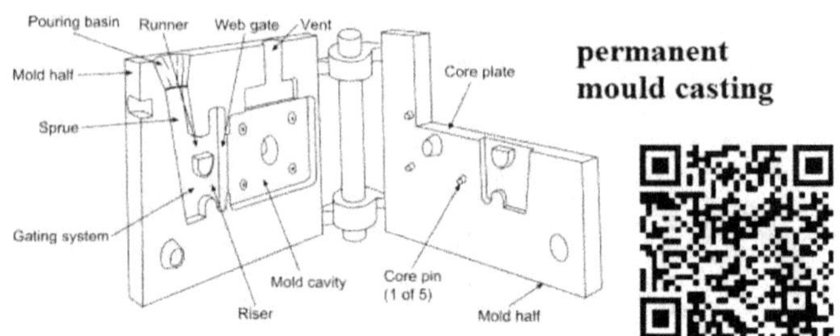

Pouring basin
Runner
Web gate
Vent
Mold half
Core plate
Sprue
Gating system
Mold cavity
Core pin
(1 of 5)
Riser
Mold half
permanent
mould casting

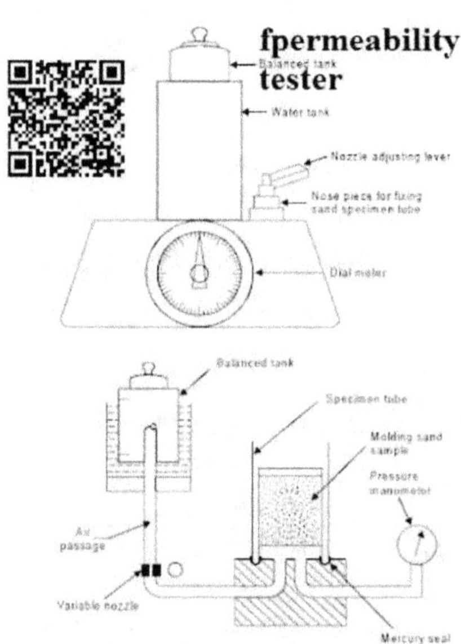

fpermeability
tester
Balanced tank
Water tank
Nozzle adjusting lever
Nose piece for fixing
sand specimen tube
Dial meter
Balanced tank
Specimen tube
Molding sand
sample
Pressure
manometer
Air
passage
Variable nozzle
Mercury seal

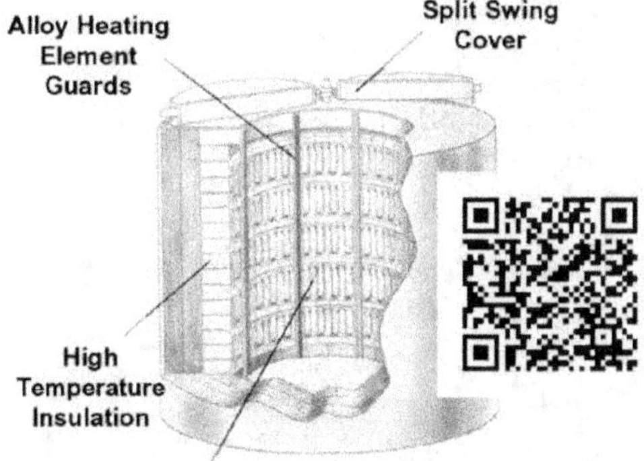

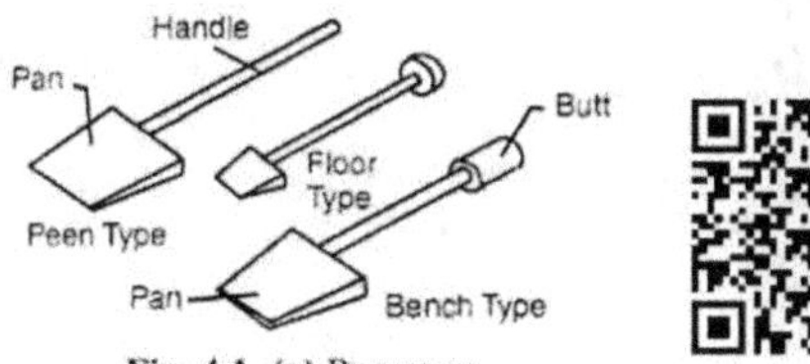

Fig. 4.1. (c) Rammers.

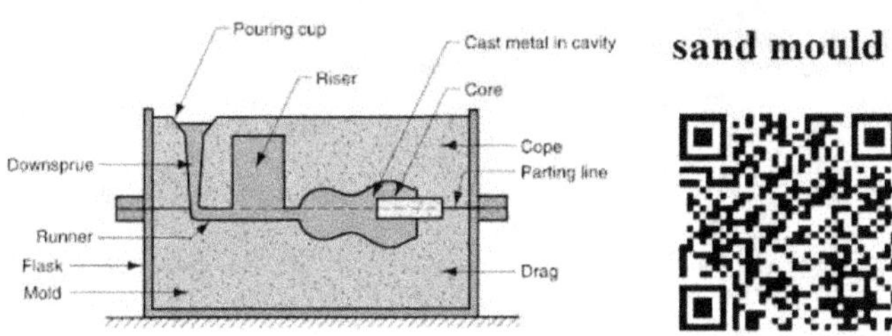

sand mould

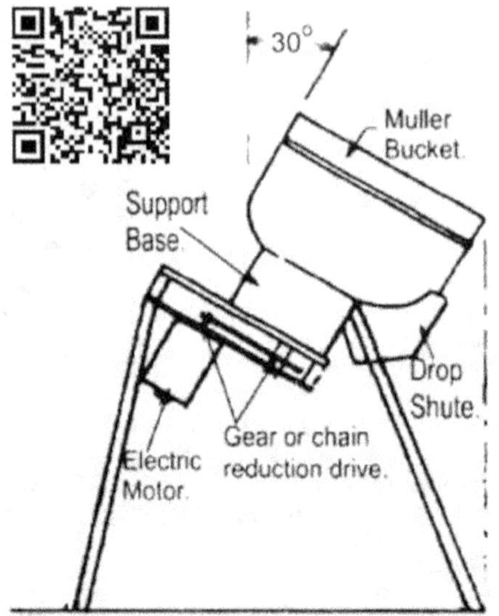

Sand Muller Gear Reduction Drive Layout.

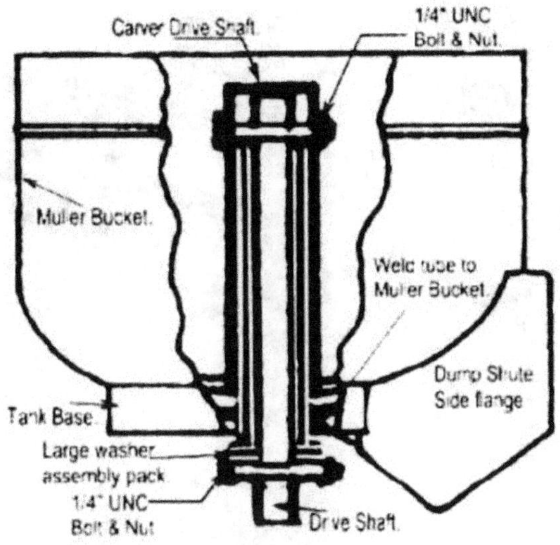

Cutaway Drawing Of Muller Assembly.

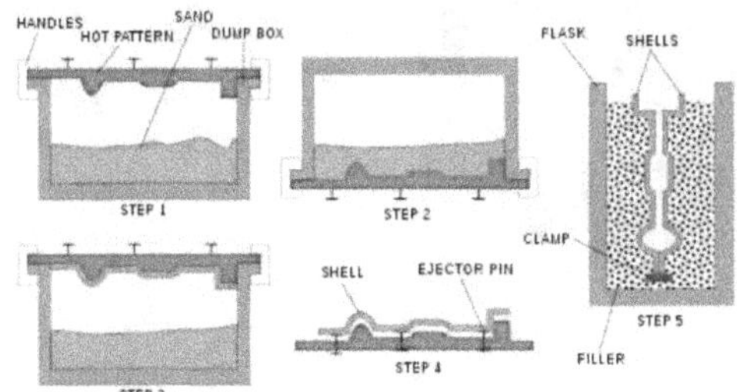

shell moulding

Parts of a
Shovel
Cutting Edge
Socket
Handle
Step
Blade
Shaft
sieve shaker
tester
DRY SAND MOULDS
Open riser
Vent
Pouring basin (cup)
Cope
Blind riser
Flask
Sprue
Sand
Core (sand)
Parting line
Drag
Mold cavity
Runner
Choke
Gate
Sand
MODI MECHANICAL ENGINEERING TUTORIALS

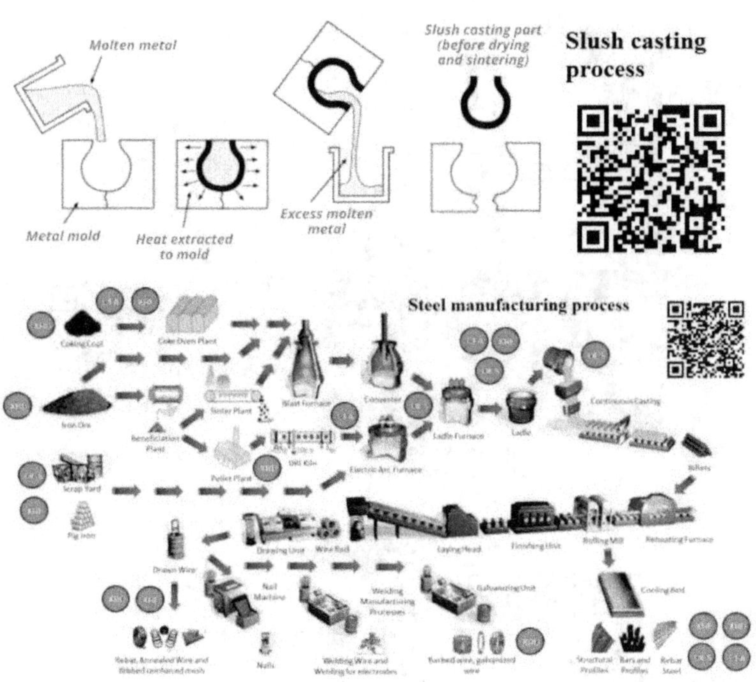

Molten metal
Metal mold
Heat extracted
to mold
Excess molten
metal
Slush casting part
(before drying
and sintering)
Slush casting
process
Steel manufacturing process

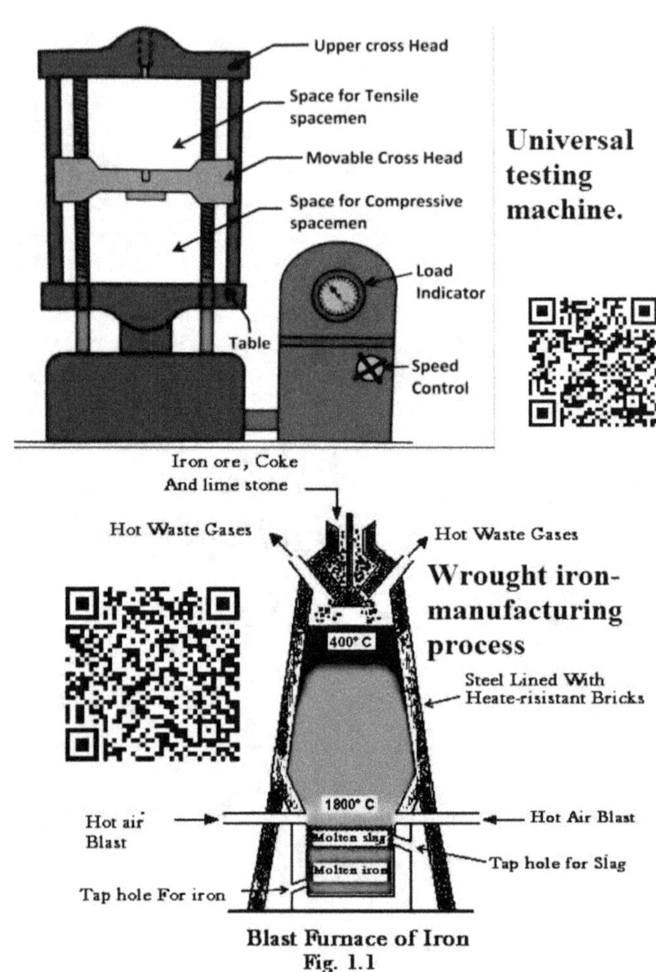

Blast Furnace of Iron
Fig. 1.1

1] Which one is a workshop safety?

<u>A] Keep shop floor clean and free from grease, oil or other slippery materials</u>

B] Stop the machine before changing the speed

C] Don't use cracked or chipped tools

D] Don't try to stop a running machine with hand

2] In Personal Protect Equipment (PPE] HELMET is used to

<u>A] protect head</u>

B] Protect eyes

C] Protect hands

D] Protect ears

3] Which of the following belongs to general safety?

A Have a worker in good attitude

B] The work clean and clear

C] Concentrate on your work

<u>D] Keep the floor and gangways clean and clear</u>

4] While grinding, which is used to protect the eyes?

A] Dark green glass

B] Mask

C] Sun glasses

<u>D] Safety goggles</u>

5] Which of the following is done for machine safety?

<u>A] Check the oil level before starting the machine</u>

B] Do things in a methodical way

C] Keep the floor and gangways clean and clear

D] Don't use dies and scarves

6] In Personal Protect Equipment (PPE], 'sleeves' is used to protect ----------

A] Face

B] Eyes

C] Ears

<u>D] Hands</u>

7] ABC stands for --------------

A] Automatic Breathing Control

B] Automatic Blood Control

<u>C] Airway Breathing Circulation</u>

D] Automatic Blood Circulation

8] Fire & FIRE EXTINGUISHERS

Fire extinguisher

9] To put off"Class B" fire, the types of fire extinguisher used is ....

A] dry power

B] Carbon dioxide

C] Jet of water

D] Foam type

10] Which type of fire extinguisher is used to put off general fire?

A] Water type Extinguisher

B] Foam type Extinguisher

C] Dry chemical powder Extinguisher

D] Carbon dioxide (C02] Extinguisher

11] In case of bleeding, take treatment Of

D] cold 3" and rest

A] spray cold water

B] Bandage immediately -----.

B] Enquire about the accident thought treatment

12] in case of an accident, the victim should im

A] Asked to take rest

C] Attended immediately

D] leave him

13] First aid is given to an injured or ill person primarily....

A] Save life

B] Prevent further deterioration of the muff's

C] Give best possible comfort

D] All of these

14] Colour code for Bins for waste paper segregation is -----

A] blue Colour

B] Yellow Colour

C] Red Colour

D] Green Colour

15] In Japanese Seiko stands for --------------

A] Shine

B] Sort

C] Standardize

D] Sustain

16] Benefit of SS system is ------

A] Increase in productivity

B] Increase in quality

C] Reduction in wastage of time

D] All of these

17] Safety is -----------

A] nobody's business

B] every bodise business

C] Some bodies business

D] The organization business

18] For basic categories of safety signs are available The meaning of"prohibition" sign ----

A] shows it must not be done

B] Shows what must be done

C] Warns the hazard or danger

D] Gives information of safety provision

18] One micrometer (U] is equal to...

A] 0.1mm

B] 0.01mm

C] 0.001mm

D] 0.0001mm

19] The caliper meant for measuring the width of a slot is...

A] Odd leg caliper

B] Outside caliper

C] Jenny caliper

D] Inside calliper

Calliper

20] The size of the dividers are specified by the -----------
A] Total length of legs
B] Distance between the points when fully opened
C] Length of legs without points
D] distance between the pivot and the point

21] The instrument used to mark parallel lines, parallel to the datum edge is -
A] jenny caliper
B] Divider
C] Outside calliper
D] Inside calliper

22] Which one of the following is an indirect measuring tool?
A] Outside caliper
B] Vernier calliper
C] Steel rule
D] Outside micrometer

23] For cutting thin tubing, the most suitable pitch of the hacksaw blade is...
A] 1.8mm
B] 1.4mm
C] 1mm
D] 0.8mm

24] For cutting solid brass, the most suitable pitch of the hacksaw blade is...
A] 1.8mm
B] 1.4mm
C] 1mm
D] 0.8mm

Hacksaw frame

25] A new hacksaw blade after a few strokes becomes loose because of the...

A] <u>Stretching of the blade</u>

B] Wing-nut threads being worn out

C] Wrong pitch of the blade

D] Improper selection of the set of saws.

26] While cutting small diameter pipes, it is advisable to watch regularly and ensure that...

A] The cut is along the curved line

B] <u>More saw teeth are in contract</u>

C] The work is not overheated

D] Proper balancing of hacksaw is maintained

27] The vice clamps are used to...

A] Protect hard jaws

B] Clamp the work pieces rigidly

C] <u>Protect the finished surfaces</u>

D] Prevent the movable jaw being filed

28] The reference surface during marking is provided by the...

A] Surface gauge

B] Workpiece

C] Drawing of the work

D] <u>Marking table surface</u>

29] The size of an engineer's vice is specified by the...

A] Length of the movable jaw

B] <u>Width of the jaws</u>

C] Height of the vice

D] Maximum opening of the jaws

30] The part of the universal surface gauge which helps to draw a parallel line along a datum edge is the..
A] Rocker arm
B] Snug
C] Fine adjustment screw
D] <u>Guide pins</u>

Universal surface guage

31] Scribers are made of...
A] Mild steel
B] <u>High carbon steel</u>
C] Brass
D] Cast iron

32] Portion of the hammer used for fixing the handle is...
A] Face
B] Peen
C] Cheek
D] <u>Eye hole</u>

33] Weight of the hammer for the marking purpose is...
A] <u>250g</u>
B] 500g
C] 1 kg
D] 2 kgs

Hammer

34] The size of the dividers are specified by the...

A] Total length of the legs

B] Distance between the points when fully opened

C] Length of legs without the points

D] <u>Distance between the pivot and the point</u>

35] The included angle of the groove of 'V' block is always....

A] 45°

B] 60°

C] 90°

D] <u>120°</u>

36] 'V' blocks are available in grades of...

A] <u>A & B</u>

B] A,B & C

C] 1,2 & 3

D] 1 & 2

37] 'V' blocks of grade 'B' are made of

A] <u>Cast iron</u>

B] Mild steel

C] Steel

D] Cast steel

38] Name the punch used to locate the centre.

A] Prick punch 30°

B] Prick punch 60°

C] <u>Centre punch</u>

D] Dot punch

Centre punch

39] The point angle of centre punch is --------

A] 30°

B] 50°

c] 900

D] 1200

40] Punches are used for forming ---------of any shape

A] Holes

B] Mining

C] Knurling

D] Reaming

41] Generally the length of the handle of the vice is ----------

A] 1.5 times the normal size of the vice

B] 2.5 times the normal size of the vice

C] 3.5 times the normal size of the vice

D] 4.5 times the normal size of the vice

Bench vice

42] Bench vice spindle is made of ....

A] mild steel

B] Cast iron

C] Tool steel

D] Bronze

43] The convexity of files helps...

A] To file concave surfaces

B] To file convex surfaces

C] To prevent rounding of edges of work

D] The file to become straight when pressure is applied

Files

44] Which file used for filling wood, leather and other soft material? .

A] Single cut file

B] Double cut file

c] Rasp cut file

D] Curved cut file

45] File used is used for ------------

A] Cleaning the work piece

C] Renewing the file teeth

B] cleaning the file teeth

D] Cleaning the chips

46] File card is used to --------

A] Clean the work piece

C] Renew the file teeth

B] Clean the file teeth

47] The point angle of scriber is -----------

A] 30°

B] 60°

C] 5° to 10°

D] 12° to 15°
48] The cutting angle for chipping cast iron is...
A] 37.5°
B] 55°
C] 60°
D] 90°

49] The chisel will dig into the material when...
A] The rake angle is more
B] The clearance angle is too low
C] The angle of inclination is more
D] The angle of inclination is too low
50] A slight convexity is given to the cutting edge to...
A] Cut curved surfaces
B] Cut sharp corners
C] Prevent digging of the ends
D] Allow the lubricant to enter
51] Surface plates are made of...
A] High grade cast steel
B] Fine-grained cast iron
C] Alloy steels
D] Wrought iron

52] Surface plates are specified by their length and breadth & are in
A] decimetre
B] Cubic meter
C] Cylindrical

53] Ribs are given on the unmachined portion of the angle plate for...
A] Easy handling
B] Convenience in manufacturing
C] Clamping while setting on machines
D] Rigidity and to prevent distortion
54] The slots on the angle plate are given for...
A] Reducing weight
B] Aligning the work
C] Lifting using hooks
D] Accommodating bolts.
55] The size of the angle plates is stated by...
A] Weight
B] Length
C] Length x width
D] Size number

Foundryman Level 1

Q 1) In terms of safety, PPE stands for
1) Personal Protective Equipment
2) Protective Personal Equipment
3) Personal Property Equipment
4) Property Protective Equipment
Q 2) Which of the following does not spread pollution?
1) Silica powder
2) Carbon dioxide
3) Oxygen
4) Dust and smoke
Q 3) Which of the following is the cause of an accident in a big industry?
1) Explosion (from furnace or molten metal)
2) Gas pollution
3) Fire
4) All of these
Q 4) A first aid box contains___________
1) Tincture of iodine
2) Burnol
3) Dettol
4) All of these
Q 5) Need of testing and inspection is required for ______________.
1) Pattern

2) Moulding sand

3) Casting

4) All of these

Q 6) The properties of foundry sand depend on its ___________.

1) Size

2) Shape

3) Grain fineness

4) All of these

Q 7) One piece pattern is called ___________ pattern.

1) Solid

2) Split

3) Sweep

4) Match plate

Q 8) Mallet is made of ___________.

1) Hard wood

2) Lead

3) Brass

4) Cast iron

Q 9) Dowel pin is used in ___________ pattern.

1) Solid

2) Two piece

3) Many pieces

4) Two piece and many pieces both

Q 10) Core box used in which of the following purpose?

1) In making a pattern

2) In making core

3) In casting

4) In ramming

Q 11) Which of the following is not an ore?

1) Hematite

2) Galena

3) Magnetite

4) Urea

Q 12) Why the taper allowance is provided on the pattern?

1) To save wood

2) To reduce the cost

3) For easy removal of the pattern from the mould

4) None of these

Q 13) Moulding sand is called ____________.

1) Silica sand

2) A mixture of silica sand, clay and water

3) Silica sand and graphite powder

4) None of these

Q 14) The mould box is usually made up of ______________.

1) Copper

2) Aluminium

3) Wood, cast iron or steel

4) None of these

Q 15) The permeability of sand mould becomes __________ by excessive ramming.

1) Less

2) More

3) No effects

4) None of these

Q 16) Which of the following is a moulding machine?

1) Jolting machine

2) Squeeze machine

3) Sand slinger

4) All of these

Q 17) Generally, the core is dried at _________ degree Celsius.

1) 80

2) 120

3) 250

4) 400

Q 18) What is the meaning of core assembly?

1) Adding or pasting two or more small portions of the core

2) Make a big core from core sand

3) Making a Big Core from Moulding Sand

4) Adding pattern and core to C-clamp

Q 19) The core is supported in the mould with the help of__________.

1) Chill

2) Chaplet

3) Rammer

4) Riser

Q 20) Which of the following is an alloy?

1) Copper

2) Iron

3) Steel

4) Aluminium

Q 21) Which of the following is a metal?

1) Brass

2) Bronze

3) Tin

4) Duralumin

Q 22) Which of the following is a non-ferrous metal?

1) Cast iron

2) Wrought iron

3) Zinc

4) Pig iron

Q 23) Cupola is used for melting __________.

1) Steel

2) Cast iron

3) Aluminium

4) Tin

Q 24) Weight of a metal is _________than it s slag weight.

1) less

2) more

3) equal

4) less and equal both

Q 25) To generate temperature in induction furnace ____________ is used.

1) Coke

2) Electric heater

3) Electric current in the copper coil

4) Electric arc

Q 26) The production of special steel in the induction furnace, ____________ element can be used.

1) Cobalt

2) Nickel

3) Chromium and Vanadium

4) All of these

Q 27) All the paths through which the melted metal comes in mould cavity, is called ______________.

1) Rising system

2) Gating system

3) Moulding system

4) None of these

Q 28) Melted metal goes through ____________ in the mould cavity.

1) Runner, sprue and ingate

2) Ingate, sprue and runner

3) Sprue, runner and ingate

4) Sprue, ingate and runner

Q 29) The part of mould that is to be cooled quickly, __________ is applied there.

1) Chill

2) Scheme bob

3) Blinder riser

4) Strainer core

Q 30) What should be kept in mind, when designing a riser?

1) Place of riser

2) Shape of riser

3) Size of riser

4) All of these

Q 31) What arrangements should be made to extinguish the fire in the workshop?

1) Firefighting equipment

2) Buckets full of water

3) Sand Buckets

4) All of these

Q 32) What is the meaning of shake out?

1) Keep clean the mould box

2) Cleaning Casting

3) After moulding, remove the sand from the mould by shaking them

4) None of these

Q 33) The action of breaking the gate and the riser from casting through the hammer is called_.

1) Removing

2) Filing

3) Flogging

4) Grinding

Q 34) Flame cutting generally uses _______________ gas.

1) Nitrogen and acetylene

2) Hydrogen and acetylene

3) Oxygen and Acetylene

4) Nitrogen and hydrogen

Q 35) Which of the following is a type of cast iron? 1) White cast iron \ सफ़ेद ढ़लवा लोहा

2) Malleable cast iron

3) Ductile cast iron

4) All of these

Q 36) The pouring cup is placed in the ___________ box

1) Drag

2) Cheek

3) Cope

4) Ladle

Q 37) The test or inspection, in which the sample is tested by breaking it, is called ___________.

1) Destructive test

2) Non-destructive test

3) Radiography test

4) None of these

Q 38) In the normalizing process, metal is cooled in________.

1) Air

2) Water

3) Oil

4) Salt Solution

Q 39) In die casting mould is made up of __________. 1) Plaster \ शिशर

2) Sand

3) Metal

4) None of these

Q 40) ___________ is used in die casting.

1) Sprue

2) Gate

3) Core

4) All of these

Q 41) Which of the following is not a type of die casting machine?

1) Hot chamber die casting machine

2) Cold chamber die casting machine

3) Water sprayed continuous die casting machine

4) All of these

Q 42) In which castings process, the molten metal is poured into a rotating mould

1) Die casting

2) Centrifugal casting

3) Carbon dioxide process

4) Shell moulding

Q 43) Carbon dioxide moulding process is also called __________ process.

1) Sodium silicate

2) Shell moulding

3) Plaster mould

4) Lost wax casting

Q 44) ____________ is easily made by slush casting method

1) Steel casting

2) Plastic glass

3) Thin jewellery

4) None of these

Q 45) The vent in a die casting is made ________.

1) To eject extra melted metal

2) To eject air or gas from the mould

3) Instead of the riser

4) None of these

Q 46) Which of the following action comes under visual inspection

1) Inspection by eyes or lens only

2) Chemical inspection

3) Inspection by Electron microscope

4) None of these

Q 47) Which of the following control chart is applicable in quality of casting?

1) X-chart

2) R-chart

3) P-chart

4) All of these

Q 48) Solid casting and blow hole contain hollow casting makes the different sound when hitting.This principle is used in __________.

1) Ultrasound test

2) Sound test

3) Radiography test

4) Test of magnetic particles

Q 49) The leak in tank or vessel in which fluid or gas is stored, can be done by ___________.

1) Sound test

2) Ultra sound test

3) Pressure test

4) Tense strength test

Q 50) Magnetic particle test is performed for _______________ casting.

1) Copper

2) Zinc

3) Iron

4) Magnesium

Q 51) The fluorescent dye test finds _______________ of casting.

1) Surface crack

2) Inner blow hole

3) Mismatch

4) Incorrect chemical structure

Q 52) Dimensional inspection is used to find out ______________.

1) To find out blow hole

2) To find out rough surface

3) To measuring the length, breadth, thickness and size

4) None of these

Q 53) ______________ is used to perform dimensional inspection.

1) Scale

2) Measuring tape

3) Slide calipers

4) All of these

Q 54) Overhead crane is used for which of the following work?

1) To carry mould box

2) Lifting ladle for casting

3) To move casting from one place to another place

4) All of these

Q 55) What is done by jolt and squeeze machine?

1) Mould making

2) Cleaning of casting

3) Making gate

4) Preparation of moulding sand

Q 56) The chutes found in the middle or end of the belt conveyor is used for _________.

1) Heating the substance

2) Dropping acidic water

3) Throwing down the moving items

4) Break substance

Q 57) In which of the following division of the foundry, there is no danger of dust pollution?

1) Moulding department

2) Fork lifter

3) Electrostatic precipitator

4) Fettling department

Q 58) Which of the following equipment reduces dust pollution?

1) Air rammer

2) Fork lifter

3) Electrostatic precipitator

4) Sand slinger

Q 59) The ___________ of the molten metal is known by the pyrometer.

1) Chemical composition

2) Temperature

3) Liquidity

4) None of these

Q 60) The computer in the foundry is used for ___________.

1) Furnace operation

2) Requirement and expense of goods

3) Annealing furnace operation

4) All of these

Q 61) Bucket elevator is used for transferring moulding substance in___________

1) Horizontal state

2) Vertical state

3) Horizontal and vertical state

4) None of these

Q 62) Test in which specimen is tested without breaking is called_______.

1) Destructive test

2) Non- Destructive test

3) Tensile strength test

4) None of these

Q 63) Which of the following test comes under non-destructive testing
1) Visual inspection
2) Impact test
3) Fluorescent-die-penetrate inspection
4) Both visual inspection and Flourescent-die-penetrate inspection
Q 64) Which one of the following is not true about moulding machine ?
1) It reduces labour costs
2) The pattern can also be removed from the mould
3) Casting is cleaned by this
4) Surface of the mould comes smooth
Q 65) Which of the following equipment is not used for making mould?
1) Jolt squeeze machine
2) Sand slinger
3) Dumper
4) None of these
Q 66) S.W.L. stands for-
1) Safe Working Load
2) Standard Working Load
3) Stable Working Load
4) Suitable Working Load
Q 67) If the volume of a casting is X cubic meters and the metal s density
of casting is Y kg. per cubic meter then its weight will be____________kg.
1) XY
2) (X/Y)
3) (Y/X)
4) None of these
Q 68) The meaning of foundry layout is ________________.
1) Cleaning / washing all materials that are to be used
2) Run smoothly metal melting furnaces
3) Show the sequence of actions used in the foundry
4) None of these
Q 69) The computer in the foundry is used for ____________.
1) Find the weight of casting
2) Cost of casting
3) Design of gate and riser
4) All of these
Q 70) Humans ________ can be affected by dust pollution.
1) Ear

2) Leg

3) Lung

4) Lever

Q 71) Which one of the following is not a related term of foundry?

1) Truing

2) Moulding

3) Core making

4) Casting

Q 72) The box which contains the usual medicine, cotton, bandage etc. is called ______ box.

1) Mould

2) Core

3) First Aid

4) Tool

Q 73) Which of the following is not a PPE?

1) Safety shoes

2) Hand gloves

3) Safety goggle

4) Pipe cutter

Q 74) Which of the following is a soft skill?

1) Strong work ethics

2) Good communication skill

3) Team work

4) All of these

Q 75) Which of the following cause is not suitable for the accident?

1) Lack of light

2) Carelessness

3) Over confidence

4) Selection of correct tool

Q 76) Which country developed 5 S system?

1) India

2) China

3) Japan

4) Germany

Q 77) Which of the following material is used in foundry?

1) Sand

2) Wood

3) Metal

4) All of these

Q 78) Which of the following metal ore name is hematite?

1) Iron

2) Aluminium

3) Copper

4) Zinc

Q 79) Which of the following is a ferrous metal?

1) Cast iron

2) Wrought iron

3) Steel

4) All of these

Q 80) Alloy of copper and zinc is known as __________.

1) Brass

2) Bronze

3) Duralumin

4) Nichrome

Q 81) Major constituent of Duralumin alloy is________________.

1) Aluminium

2) Copper

3) Zinc

4) Iron

Q 82) Which of the following is not a ferrous metal?

1) Copper

2) Zinc

3) Both copper and zinc

4) Steel

Q 83) Which one of the following metals has better electrical conductivity than copper ?

1) Silver

2) Tin

3) Zinc

4) Lead

Q 84) The property of metal by which it can be drawn into wires is called__________.

1) conductivity

2) malleability

3) ductility

4) elasticity

Q 85) Which of the following is ingredient of moulding sand?
1) Silica sand
2) Clay
3) Water
4) All of these

Q 86) The property of moulding sand that allow gases to pass through is called as ___________.
1) chemical resistance
2) permeability
3) durability
4) conductivity

Q 87) Which of the following is not a core sand ingredient?
1) Water
2) Wax
3) Core sand binder
4) Silica sand

Q 88) Top box of the moulding box is called as ______.
1) Cope
2) Cheek
3) Drag
4) Core

Q 89) The projection provided on the patterns for the seating of the core is known as _______.
1) core print
2) core box
3) core spring
4) core chill

Q 90) Which of the following is a type of reinforcement used for cores?
1) Spring
2) Arbor
3) Gagger
4) All of these

Q 91) Core venting is done to________ the permeability of the core.
1) improve
2) stop
3) decrease
4) degrade

Q 92) The vertical portion of the gating system, which is adjacent to the pouring cup, is called _______.

1) runner

2) sprue

3) riser

4) channel

Q 93) The _______defect occurs when cope and drag have not properly aligned.

1) mis-run

2) cold shut

3) mould shift

4) scab

Q 94) Which of the following defect occur due to insufficient fluidity of the molten metal?

1) Mis-run

2) Mould shift

3) Blow hole

4) None of these

Q 95) Type of testing or inspection in which casting is tested without breaking is called _________.

1) non-destructive testing

2) destructive testing

3) semi-destructive testing

4) None of these

Q 96) The operation of cutting of the unwanted parts, cleaning and finishing of the casting is called

___________.

1) ramming

2) fetlling

3) jolting

4) slinging

Q 97) Which of the following property of metal is affected by heat treatment?

1) Hardness

2) Ductility

3) Strength

4) All of these

Q 98) Electric arc furnace is used for melting of _______.

1) steel
2) aluminium
3) copper
4) zinc
Q 99) Electrode in the electric arc furnace is made up of _____.
1) copper
2) aluminium
3) graphite
4) steel
Q 100) Which of the following is a part of cupola furnace?
1) Bottom plate
2) Shell
3) Propping rod
4) All of these
Q 101) Core type induction furnace is a __________ frequency induction furnace.
1) high
2) low
3) medium
4) zero
Q 102) Melting point of iron is approximately_________ degree centigrate.
1) 1000
2) 723
3) 1539
4) 4000
Q 103) Which of the following is a developed form of cupola ?
1) Coke less cupola
2) Hot blast cupola
3) Divide blast cupola
4) All of these
Q 104) Which of the following is not a type of cast iron?
1) White cast iron
2) Malleable cast iron
3) Ductile cast iron
4) Yellow cast iron
Q 105) Identify the tool shown in the figure.
1) Try square

2) File

3) Chisel

4) Steel rule

Q 106) The process of making the mould with the help of moulding machine is known as __________.

1) machine moulding

2) core machining

3) basic moulding

4) fettling

Q 107) Which of the following is not an advantage of machine moulding?

1) High production rate

2) High dimensional accuracy

3) The initial cost of equipments are high.

4) It provides good surface finish to mould and casting

Q 108) Which of the following is a hand operated moulding machine?

1) Plain stripper type machine

2) Push off type machine

3) Roll over type machine

4) All of these

Q 109) Which of the following is not a core ramming machine?

1) Jolting

2) Slinging

3) Squeezing

4) Small bench blower

Q 110) Which of the following is a type of die casting machine?

1) Hot chamber die casting machine

2) Cold chamber die casting machine

3) Goose-neck die casting machine

4) All of these

Q 111) Sodium silicate moulding process is also called __________ process.

1) Carbon di oxide moulding

2) Shell moulding

3) Plaster mould

4) Lost wax casting

Q 112) Which of the following die casting machine has a suitable furnace for melting and holding the metal?

1) Hot chamber die casting machine

2) Cold chamber die casting machine

3) Water sprayed continuous die casting machine

4) None of these

Q 113) The mould becomes stiff due to the formation of _______ in the sodium silicate process.

1) sodium carbonate

2) silica gel

3) calcium carbonate

4) Carbon di oxide

Q 114) Shell moulding can be used for_________.

1) producing milling cutter

2) producing gear

3) producing thick wall casting

4) producing thin wall casting

Q 115) The mould in plaster of paris mould casting is made of ______.

1) gypsum

2) glass

3) sodium silicate

4) graphite

Q 116) Which department is definitely in the good layout of a foundry?

1) Moulding department

2) Fettling department

3) Inspection department

4) All of these

Q 117) Which department of foundry decides that casting is in line with the prescribed standards?

1) Moulding department

2) Fettling department

3) Inspection department

4) Core making department

Q 118) Which of the following is a material handling equipment used in a mechanized foundry?

1) Crane

2) Conveyor

3) Both crane and conveyor

4) None of these

Q 119) Which of the following material handling equipment is used to pour molten metal into mould in a mechanized foundry?

1) Truck
2) Belt conveyor
3) Ladle crane
4) Tractor
Q 120) Which of the following is not a type of conveyor?
1) Belt conveyor
2) Roller conveyor
3) Pallet conveyor
4) None of these
Q 121) Which of the following material is transported through material handling equipments in a mechanized foundry?
1) Moulding sand
2) Molted metal
3) Casting
4) All of these
Q 122) Which of the following instrument is used for dimensional inspection?
1) Vernier caliper
2) Limit gauge
3) Steel rule
4) All of these
Q 123) Identify the instrument shown in the figure.
1) Vernier caliper
2) Limit gauge
3) Micrometer
4) Steel rule
Q 124) Which quality of material can be tested with the help of rockwell and brinell test?
1) Hardness
2) Malleability
3) Elasticity
4) Ductility
Q 125) Tensile testing is a type of____________.
1) non-destructive testing
2) destructive testing
3) semi-destructive testing
4) visual inspection
Q 126) Tensile test can be performed on_______.

1) Universal testing machine

2) Izod tester

3) Rockwell tester

4) Brinell tester

Q 127) What type of defects are detected by pressure test?

1) Scab

2) Leak

3) Mis-run

4) None of these

Q 128) Salvaging can be done by which of the following method?

1) Thermit welding

2) Electric arc welding

3) Brazing

4) All of these

Q 129) Which of the following test is also called X-Ray test?

1) Ultrasonic test

2) Sound test

3) Radiography test

4) Test of magnetic particles

Q 130) Which of the following metal casting can be tested by magnetic particle inspection?

1) Aluminium

2) Zinc

3) Iron

4) Sodium

Q 131) _________ test is based on the principle of reflection of high frequency sound waves.

1) Pressure test

2) Impact test

3) Radiography test

4) Ultrasonic test

Q 132) In fluorescent dye penetrant test, the penetrant passes into cracks by________ action.

1) capillary

2) friction

3) radiation

4) conduction

Q 133) When statistical techniques are employed to control, improve and maintain the quality or to solve qualityproblems it is called __________.

1) Advanced quality control

2) Basic quality control

3) Statistical quality control

4) Quality pack

Q 134) Which of the following machine should be installed at the place of dust pollution?

1) Shake out machine

2) Jolting machine

3) Electrostatic precipitator

4) Sand slinger

Q 135) Which one of the following is a type of pollution?

1) Air pollution

2) Noise pollution

3) Water pollution

4) All of these

Q 136) What cost should be kept in mind when calculating the total cost of casting?

1) Material cost

2) Labour cost

3) Overhead cost

4) All of these

Q 137) Why quality control is needed in foundries?

1) To reduce production cost

2) To reduce inspection cost

3) To reduce both production and inspection cost

4) None of these

Q 138) In which section of foundry should the quality be taken care of?

1) Mould making section

2) Fettling section

3) Melting section

4) All of these

Q 139) Which of the following protection equipment prevents dust particles from entering the lungs?

1) Hand gloves

2) Safety shoes

3) Nose mask

4) Apron

Q 140) Which of the following term is related to foundry?

1) Truing

2) Moulding

3) Nibbling

4) Glazing

Q 141) Identify the tool shown in the figure.

1) Try square

2) File

3) Chisel

Answer Key

Level 1 Answer key

Question No.	Option	Question No.	Option	Question No.	Option	Question No.	Option	Question No.	Option
1	1	31	4	61	2	91	1	121	4
2	3	32	3	62	2	92	2	122	4
3	4	33	3	63	4	93	3	123	1
4	4	34	3	64	3	94	1	124	1
5	4	35	4	65	3	95	1	125	2
6	4	36	3	66	1	96	2	126	1
7	1	37	1	67	1	97	4	127	2
8	1	38	1	68	3	98	1	128	4
9	4	39	3	69	4	99	3	129	3
10	2	40	4	70	3	100	4	130	3
11	4	41	3	71	1	101	2	131	4
12	3	42	2	72	3	102	3	132	1
13	2	43	1	73	4	103	4	133	3
14	3	44	3	74	4	104	4	134	3
15	1	45	2	75	4	105	4	135	4

16	4	46	1	76	3	106	1	136	4
17	3	47	4	77	4	107	3	137	3
18	1	48	2	78	1	108	4	138	4
19	2	49	3	79	4	109	4	139	3
20	3	50	3	80	1	110	4	140	2
21	3	51	1	81	1	111	1	141	2
22	3	52	3	82	3	112	1		
23	2	53	4	83	1	113	2		
24	2	54	4	84	3	114	4		
25	3	55	1	85	4	115	1		
26	4	56	3	86	2	116	4		
27	2	57	3	87	2	117	3		
28	3	58	3	88	1	118	3		
29	1	59	2	89	1	119	3		
30	4	60	4	90	4	120	4		

4) Steel rule

Q 1) Which metal ore is bauxite?

1) Copper

2) Aluminium

3) Iron

4) None of these

Q 2) What is the meaning of preparation of moulding sand?

1) Mixing moulding sand and core sand

2) Mixing the moulding sand ingredients together

3) Proper ramming of moulding sand

4) All of these

Q 3) Which of the following tools does not use to make the mould?

1) Rammer

2) Cleaner or Lifter

3) Gaggers

4) Crucible

Q 4) What to do for increasing the strength of core while making the core?

1) It is heated

2) The rod or wire is inserted in the middle of the core
3) The core is situated in the mould and left for a while
4) None of these
Q 5) Which of the following is a Pit furnace?
1) Electric Arc Furnace
2) Rotary Furnace
3) Crusible Furnace
4) None of these
Q 6) Which of the following is not a type of gate?
1) Top gate
2) Parting line gate
3) Bottom gate
4) Middle gate
Q 7) Which of the following is a personal protective equipmet ?
1) Rammer
2) Sprit level
3) Mask
4) Riser
Q 9) Which of the following process can be overcome by the internal force generated in casting?
1) Annealing
2) Quenching
3) Nitriding
4) Normalizing
Q 10) Which of the following process does not comes under heat treatment?
1) Annealing
2) Quenching
3) Tempering
4) Sand blasting
Q 11) In which of the following method a metal is cooled in salt solution after heating?
1) Annealing
2) Stress relieving
3) Normalising
4) Quenching
Q 12) Which of the following methods is used for surface hardening?
1) Induction hardening

2) Flame hardening

3) Resistance heating hardening

4) All of these

Q 13) In the investment casting process, mould is made up of which of the following material?

1) Plaster

2) Graphite

3) Wax

4) None of these

Q 14) Which of the following is a test to check hardness?

1) Izod test

2) Charpy test

3) Brinell test

4) All of these

Q 15) Which one of the following rays are used to test thick casting?

1) X-Ray

2) Gamma-ray

3) Alpha-ray

4) None of these

Q 16) Which of the following items is not used in a mechanized foundry?

1) Jolting machine

2) Belt conveyors

3) Wooden rammer

4) Squeeze machine

Q 17) Which of the following work can be done for foundry using the robot?

1) For the transfer of foundry substances

2) For safety related tasks

3) In the department of metal melting

4) All of these

Q 18) What is the use of belt conveyors in foundry?

1) For mixing the moulding sand

2) For transferring moulding sand vertically upward

3) For making core

4) For transferring moulding sand horizontally one place to other place upward

Q 19) Which of the following test is a Destructive test ?

1) Pressure test

2) Ultrasonic test

3) Gamma-ray test

4) None of these

Q 20) Which of the following should be taken into consideration, if the value of casting is to be calculated?

1) The costs in forming patterns, cores and moulds

2) The cost in melting metal

3) Fettling expenses and benefits

4) All of these

Q 21) If the density of a casting is 80 kg.per cubic meter and its volume is 40 cubic meters. What will be the weight of the casting in kilogram?

1) 2

2) 20

3) 320

4) 3200

Q 22) What will be the difference between the layout of cast iron foundry and steel foundry?

1) In mould making instrument

2) In core making instrument

3) In melted furnaces

4) In shake out machine

Q 23) Which of the following should be installed at the workplace where smoke and dust particles fly?

1) Generator

2) Bessemer

3) Exhauster

4) Hydro blasting machine

Q 24) Which heat treatment should be done to remove the internal stress of steel castings?

1) Annealing

2) Normalizing

3) Quenching

4) Tempering and Quenching

Q 25) Which sand is used to fill up the mould after applying facing sand?

1) Core sand

2) Zircon sand

3) Baking sand

4) None of these

Q 26) Which of the following is an alloy of carbon and iron?
1) Aluminium
2) Copper
3) Steel
4) Brass

Q 27) Which of the following is a special additive of moulding sand?
1) Coal dust
2) Silica flour
3) Cow dung
4) All of these

Q 28) Which of the following material can be used for making pattern?
1) Metal
2) Wood
3) Both metal and wood
4) None of these

Q 29) Identify the pattern shown in the figure.
1) Solid pattern
2) Sweep pattern
3) Match plate pattern
4) None of these

Q 30) What is the another name of tapper allowance?
1) Rapping allowance
2) Draft allowance
3) Machining allowance
4) Camber allowance

Q 31) Which of the following is not a type of core?
1) Horizontal core
2) Vertical core
3) Kiss core
4) None of these

Q 32) Which of the following is not a part of gating system?
1) riser
2) runner
3) pouring cup
4) barrel

Q 33) What is the name of riser which have the head open towards the atmosphere?
1) Open riser

2) Blind riser

3) Close riser

4) None of these

Q 34) Which one of the following is a type of core box?

1) Half core box

2) Split core box

3) Gang core box

4) All of these

Q 35) Which heat treatment is done on steel to increase its cutting ability?

1) Annealing

2) Hardening

3) Tempering

4) Normalising

Q 36) In normalising, cooling is done in which of the following medium?

1) Oil

2) Water

3) Air

4) Brine

Q 37) Which of the following furnace is also called as air furnace?

1) Reverberatory furnace

2) Electric arc furnace

3) Cupola furnace

4) Induction furnace

Q 38) Which furnace is used for melting small quantity of non ferrous metal?

1) Cupola furnace

2) Electric arc furnace

3) Pit furnace

4) None of these

Q 39) Pyrometer is used for measuring which of the following quantity?

1) Pressure

2) Temperature

3) Flow

4) Volume

Q 40) Which of the following processes produce casting when pressure forces the molten metal to go into the mould cavity?

1) Shell moulding

2) Die casting

3) Continuous casting

4) Carbon dioxide moulding

Q 41) Which casting is used for making ornament, statues, toys?

1) Die casting

2) Centrifugal casting

3) Slush casting

4) None of these

Q 42) What indenter is used for Brinell test?

1) Hardened steel ball

2) Diamond ball

3) Diamond prism

4) Steel prism

Q 43) Which of the following instrument is used in sound test?

1) Stethoscope

2) Laser

3) Manometer

4) None of these

Q 44) Which of the following is not a method of preparation of defective areas in salvaging?

1) Grinding

2) Gouging

3) Rolling

4) Chipping

Q 45) Which of the following is produced in the form of slags in thermite welding?

1) Iron

2) Aluminium oxide

3) Zinc oxide

4) Silica

Q 46) In heat treatment processes which of the following has the slowest rate of cooling?

1) Air

2) Oil

3) Water

4) Brine

Q 47) Which of the following is a heat treatment process of metals?

1) Annealing

2) Normalising
3) Tempering
4) All of these
Q 48) Which of the following is a surface hardening process?
1) Annealing
2) Nitriding
3) Tempering
4) Normalising
Q 49) What kind of advanced testing process is X-ray diffraction analysis?
1) Non-destructive testing
2) Destructive testing
3) Semi-destructive testing
4) None of these
Q 50) Which of the following is a use of industrial computed tomography?
1) Flaw detection
2) Failure analysis
3) Metrology
4) All of these
Q 51) Which of the following is a type of control chart?
1) X -bar chart
2) R-chart
3) Both X -bar chart and R-chart
4) None of these
Q 52) If the density of a casting is 750 kg per cubic meter and its volume is 5 cubic meters. What will be the weight of the casting in kilogram?
1) 15
2) 375
3) 3750
4) 15000

Level 2 Answer key

Question No.	Option	Question No.	Option
1	2	31	4
2	2	32	4
3	4	33	1
4	2	34	4
5	3	35	2
6	4	36	3
7	3	37	1
8	1	38	3
9	1	39	2
10	4	40	2
11	4	41	3
12	4	42	1
13	3	43	1
14	3	44	3
15	2	45	2

16	3	46	1
17	4	47	4
18	4	48	2
19	4	49	1
20	4	50	4
21	4	51	3
22	3	52	3
23	3		
24	1		
25	3		
26	3		
27	4		
28	3		
29	3		
30	2